How to Make a Budget Plan
Planning and Budgeting for Success

Science of Living Series
M. Usman

Mendon Cottage Books

JD-Biz Publishing

Our books are available at

1. Amazon.com
2. Barnes and Noble
3. Itunes
4. Kobo
5. Smashwords
6. Google Play Books

Download Free Books!
http://MendonCottageBooks.com

Table of Contents

Preface

Do you always run out of money before your next paycheck arrives? Chances are you do get enough money, but fail to manage it. Specifically, you don't make a budget. You are among the 66% of the population who believe budgeting is difficult and a waste of time. However, if you really want to get the most from your money, you can't toss budgeting out of your life.

Years ago, I noticed I was having difficulty keeping up with my expenses. Every penny I would get would fly out of my wallet in a blink of an eye. As a result, I started borrowing. But this only made things worse.

Eventually, I learned about budgeting and its benefits. I was reluctant at first but I still gave it a shot. Within months, my financial situation improved. I was in control of my money unlike before.

So here I am. And I can't imagine a life without a budget plan. I would feel like I'm trying to invade an army of aliens without weapons.

In this book, I will share with you the benefits of budgeting. Not only that, but I will also show you how to create a budget plan. You will also find tips on increasing your income, getting out of debt, and more. I'm sure you will find the book beneficial.

Enjoy the reading!

Chapter 1: Budgeting 101

Everyone's life is driven by needs. Perhaps, you want a new smartphone, new clothes, money to pay for rent, etc. If you look closely, you will realize that you have a lot of needs. In fact, you would describe them as unlimited. Unfortunately, it's your income that's limited, and it determines whether you can afford to buy that new phone or not.

Your income forces you to make choices on which of your needs you will pursue.

A budget plan is a tool that ensures you've chosen the right needs to spend your money on. Budgeting helps you balance your expenditure with your income. If you skimp on it, you risk spending more than you earn. And this can lead to problems.

Unlike budgets for organizations, yours doesn't have to be a bunch of pages. As long as it gives a clear picture of your income, as well as expenses, you have nothing to worry about.

Importance of Budgeting

Many think budgeting is a waste of time. They believe the effort it needs is not justifiable. However, saying budgeting is important is an understatement. Here are some of its benefits:

You avoid wasteful spending – track your expenses for a month and you'll be shocked to see the things that eat your money. A cup of coffee on the way to work may not seem like much. But in 30 days, it can add up. A budget helps you to only spend on things that matter.

Keeps you out of debt – being in a debt is not fun. The lingering feeling that somebody will go to any length unitl you give him back his money is depressing. Without a budget, the risk of getting into a debt is very real. And you may have trouble getting out of it.

Can help you save – ever since you were a kid, you learned about the importance of saving. But now that you are grown up and you make your own money, you may find it hard to save. Paying for gas, electricity, food, rent, and other things will leave less in your pocket. But when you make a budget, you may become successful at saving.

You achieve your goals – money is foundational in life. But like I said earlier, it is never enough. Budgeting gives you a chance to only use your money for things that matter, enabling you to achieve your goals. These could be buying a house, a new car, paying for college, etc.

You have a better life – this is an overlooked benefit of budgeting. When you create a budget, you anticipate problems. So you can make plans on how you will deal with them. Not only does this eliminate nasty surprises, but it can also prevent stress that comes with lack of financial freedom.

What's the Best Duration for a Budget?

Your budget should show how you will spend money over a long time. Ideally, it must show expenses and incomes for at least a year. However, the biggest problem with this is that the future is not predictable. So long-term budgets usually prove inaccurate. Additionally, you cannot add the little expenses in this kind of a budget.

As a solution, you must have another budget. This will show your monthly expenses and incomes. This will help you account for things like coffee, weekend outings, movies you buy, etc.

Chapter 2: Tips for Tracking Your Expenses

Budgeting is about balancing your incomes with expenses.

If you have a day job, you know your income because you see it on your payslip. If you have a business, you also know how much you take home. It's the expenses that may be a bit of a problem. And without knowing them, you can't make a good budget.

To know how much you spend per month, you need to track your expenses for at least 30 days. As you do this, you must avoid taking shortcuts. Tracking expenses is a lot of work and there is no other way to it. It needs perseverance.

A common mistake is to estimate your expenses. This leads to budget plans that are out of touch with reality. In fact, such budgets are as good as not making one in the first place.

To record your expenses, you need a notebook or a piece of paper and a pen. Alternatively, you can use a note-taking app downloaded into your smartphone. If you know another way you can use, go for it as long as it helps you know where your money is going.

Types of Expenses

Expenses come in two forms: essential and nonessential expenses. I'm sure the names are self-explanatory. When budgeting, you need to give much priority to the essential type. Extra income should go to non-essentials expenses.

Another thing to know is that the above types of expenses can further be divided into fixed and variable expenses.

Fixed expenses do not change regardless of how much you use them. For example, you will still pay the same amount for rent whether you sleep in your house for 3 days, 10 days, or 30 days.

On the other hand, variable expenses change depending on usage. If you say you won't eat for a month, you will not spend any money on food. So your food expenses for that month will be zero. The distinction between fixed and variable expenses will help you make estimates when making your budget.

Examples

Essential expenses

- food
- gas

- phone
- rent
- house maintenance
- medical bills
- savings, etc.

Nonessential Expenses

- books
- magazines
- clothes
- games
- gifts
- vacation
- gym membership, etc.

Tips for Tracking Expenses

Here are some things you should keep in mind when trying to figure out your expenses daily:

Don't focus on categorizing – when you are collecting your expenses every day, try not get into the labor of categorizing them. Instead, just write them down. This will save you time and keep your morale high. You can categorize the expenses at the end of the day. Or if you feel like, you may even do it at the end of the month.

Record every cost – many like to only record high-dollar expenses. But this is a mistake. You will end up with a total that is not real. In the end, you will discover that you are having trouble staying within your budget.

So make sure you keep every receipt, no matter how cheap the item is. When buying online, make sure you record the money spent on each transaction. If you lose money, record it too.

Here is the rule – for every penny that goes out of your pocket, ensure that you record it. And remember to include dates too.

Start by estimating your expenses – I have found that it's useful to first estimate all my expenses before I get into the labor of tracking them. This is especially helpful with fixed expenses.

Chapter 3: How to Make a Budget

Making a budget is simple. And it's stupid to think you need an accounting degree to be good at it. The only problem is that budgeting takes time. And in some cases, you may have to work with a lot of information, which can be exhausting.

In this chapter, I will show you how easy budgeting is.

Guide to Creating a Budget

You first need to determine your income. As stated in the last chapter, this is easy. If you have a day job, simply look at your payslip. If you're a business person, the money you take for personal use is your income. In fact, income is any money you get that you can use for personal needs.

Next, you need to know your expenses. I also showed how you can do this

---

in the last chapter. So by making a budget, I assume you have tracked your expenses for at least 30 days.

You now need to bring all the expenses together. This is also the best time to categorize them and add the similar ones. For example, you may have records for gas you have been buying for a whole month. Add these so you have one figure. Although this can seem like a lot of work, it will make your work less messy.

Once done, you can go on to create the actual budget.

If you like to go old school, you are free to use a pen and a piece of paper. Alternatively, you can go for online budgeting programs like Mvelops, Quicken, or Mint.

But in this chapter, we will assume you are using a spreadsheet.

Your budget needs 3 sections. The first should show your incomes, the second should detail your expenses, and the third should have totals of your incomes and expenses.

Also, the budget must have 3 columns. These should be labeled:

1. Detail - gives names of expenses or incomes
2. Estimated – shows values of what you **thought** each item in your budget would be.
3. Actual – shows the actual income you earned or the actual cost you incurred.

Let me clarify this with an example:

> *Cathy lives by herself and works as a maid. She now wants to make a budget for the month of February. After reading this book, she now knows that she first needs to determine her income and expenses.*

As a maid, she makes $1,000 a month. Additionally, she has a blog that makes her $400 per month. She has managed to track her expenses from 1 January to 31 January. Here is what she has come up with:

Food - $200
Rent - $800
Gas - $50
Clothes - $30
Healthy insurance - $50
Cable TV - $50
Phone bills - $40
Electricity bill - $50
Water bill -$18

Now she wants to make a budget for the month of February. Here is how she can do it.

Cathy's Budget for the Month of February

	Details	Estimated	Actual
Incomes	Maid	1,000	1,000
	Blog	400	300
	Total	**1,400**	**1,300**
Expenses	Rent	800	800
	Clothes	30	35
	Gasoline	50	48
	Healthy insurance	50	50
	Cable TV	50	50
	Phone bill	40	41
	Electricity bill	50	50
	Water bill	18	17
	Food	200	205
	Total	**1,288**	**1,296**
Results	Total Monthly Income	1,400	1,300
	Total Monthly Expense	1,288	1,296
	Variance	**112**	**4**

The values in the "Estimated" column are written at the beginning of the month while the "Actual" column gets its values at the end of the month.

Looking at the "Estimated" column, Cathy should be happy since her expenses are less than her income.

But at the end of the month (actual column), she has $1,296 in expenses, which is more than the $1,288 she had estimated. Thankfully, $1,296 is still below her income for that month, which is $1,300. She will have a reminder of $4 in February.

What to Do When Expenses Are Greater Than Your Income

Imagine this situation:

Cathy is making her budget for February. And she has added *another item to the expenses that costs $212. So her total estimated expenses now make $1,500. But we know that her estimated income is $1,400. So she is down by $100.*

Whenever your income is less than your expenses, you have a problem. However, there are a couple of solutions to this.

Substitute – if you can think a little, you should find alternatives to the things on your expenses list that are cheaper. For example, instead of hiring a babysitter, you can ask a friend to give you a hand. If you buy gifts, you can start making them at home. You may also rent a cheaper house.

Remove other things from your expenses – if you have other expenses that are non-essential, you can get rid of them. You will reintroduce them in your life when you'll be able to afford them. These may include magazines, movies, money for vacations, new clothes, etc.

Reduce some expenses – some costs can be reduced. For instance, instead of dining out, you can cook at home. Instead of hiring an experienced worker to help you with something, you can opt for someone who is new in the game. Also, you can use energy efficient bulbs to save on electricity.

Use preventative measures – they say prevention is better than cure. But I say prevention is cheaper than cure. Some expenses are a result of reckless living.

If you eat junk, you are bound to gain weight and suffer the consequences. You should spend money on health books, exercising gear, and gym membership.

The same is the case if you indulge in bad behaviors like smoking, drug abuse, binge drinking, reckless driving, etc.

Borrow – usually, this should be the last option. Once you get into debt, it can be hard to get out of it. So when borrowing, borrow only what you need.

Make more money – this is probably the best way to make sure you have enough money to cover your budget. I have shared a list of things you can do to make more money in Chapter 5.

Chapter 4: Common Budgeting Mistakes to Avoid

When new to something, it's easy to fall into potholes. Budgeting is no exception. However, what you must know is that others have been there and have done that. So you don't have to learn from your mistakes. Rather, learn from theirs.

Here is the list of mistakes you should avoid when making a budget plan:

1. Neglecting Irregular Expenses

Some expenses will only come once, twice, or three times a year. Nonetheless, these expenses must be included in your budget. Since they may not occur now, it means you must estimate them. Once done, you should make an allowance that contributes to such expenses every month. Not only will this make the expense less of a burden, but you will also avoid going broke when it comes.

2. Being Misled By Your Peers

We are all different and it's important that we stay true to ourselves. If you can't afford something, try to resist the urge to spend money on it just because your friends are. Actually, trying to live like someone who earns more than you is a guaranteed way to blow your budget. And it's also guaranteed to get you into a debt.

3. Not saving any money

It's important to save some money, no matter how little you earn. Think of it, if you are are dedicated to saving each month, in 5 or 10 years, you may have enough to buy a house or even a car.

Also, saving means you will have your own personal bank. When you want to make an investment, you will avoid borrowing from traditional banks. Additionally, saving your money at a bank will make it grow through interest.

4. Not consulting your partner

If you are married, chances are that you bring your income and that of your partner in one place. In that case, I don't need to tell you how important it is to make your budget together with your spouse. This will ensure that you are both committed to staying within spending limits.

But even if your partner contributes no income, it's still important that you involve her in the budgeting process. It's not like you are the only one who'll spend the money - your partner will be involved too.

5. Having Unrealistic Expectations

We all like to have good expectations about the future. But sometimes, these good dreams can get filled with hype. And that's a problem when it comes to budgeting.

For example, in an effort to lower your expenses, you may convince yourself that some expenses will not happen that month when you know deep down that there is no chance of eliminating such expenses. So you would end up with a budget that's less than your actual expenses.

Another problem is the expectation that you will earn more. This can again lead to problems since your actual earnings may be less. So when making your estimations, try to be as realistic as possible. Although this is not easy, you should force it on yourself as it is very important.

Chapter 5: Ways to Make More Money

For most of us, even if we would increase our income, we still wouldn't be able to buy everything we want. But then, we would be able to buy most of the things we want. And as a bonus, we would have more financial security.

Unfortunately, making money is hard. If it wasn't, everyone would be rich. In this chapter, I will share tips you can use to make more money.

Freelancing

It won't make you rich overnight. And it may not earn you enough to quit your day job. But you'll enjoy it as you will be doing something you love. This could be writing, photography, designing, or anything. Also, you can freelance along with your day job.

However, getting a foothold in freelancing is tough. And you will make peanuts when getting started. During this time, your focus should be on making a name for yourself and having reliable clients.

For quicker results, start by investing in developing yourself. If you want to do freelance writing, for example, take a couple of writing courses. Not only will these make you win jobs faster, but you will also gain the necessary knowledge.

Start a Website
Don't start a website thinking it will pay the bills this month. It takes time to build traffic. And it takes even longer to start making money.

Creating a website is easy, but it's the work that follows that determines your success.

You should focus your website in a niche with low competition. This will make it easy for you to rank in search results. Doing keyword research should give you a good list of low competition niches. Once you choose a niche, make great content that will wow your visitors.

As for monetizing your website, you have a number of options. These include affiliate marketing, PPC advertising, selling your own products, etc.

Start a Business
If you have the funds, you can even start a small business in your area. Examples include selling wedding cakes, cleaning houses, cleaning cars, and growing vegetables.

But before you start your business, ensure you have a business plan. This will help determine if your business idea is viable. Additionally, remember to advertise the moment you open the business's doors.

Change Careers

If you believe you chose a wrong career path, it's not too late to jump ship. Unfortunately, this may not bring you money right away. In fact, you will need to do some hard work before you will get to your greener pasture.

For a start, take time to evaluate your new career path. Does it have enough demand? How tough is the competition? Will you earn more than what you are already getting? You can think of other questions you believe are important.

If you decide that making the switch is worth it, you still need to do some things. Most importantly, you need skills that will help your excel at your new job. And most of the times, this means more training.

Change Jobs

Sometimes, it may not be a wrong career path - you may simply be working for a not-so-generous organization. In this case, look for a job elsewhere.

But as you will be doing this, you need to think about the importance of upgrading your skills. It will make you competitive, increasing chances of getting a job in another organization. At the same time, it should also lead to better pay.

Ask for a Raise

If you believe you deserve more than what you are currently earning, it makes sense to ask your boss for a raise. And this is easier than looking for another job or changing careers.

The only problem you must overcome is your fear. A good percentage of employees fail to ask for a raise fearing their boss will get mad. So they sit in silence and complain for years.

Rent your things

You may have something you are not using. Instead of watching it sit, let it make you money. For example, you can rent your car or parking space. And that is easy since you don't need to put in any real effort.

You may also provide accommodation to travelers if you have free rooms in your house. Depending on where you live, you can make a lot of money with this. The only drawback is that you will be letting strangers into your house.

Teach Your Skills

You may be good at playing piano, sewing, fixing broken phones, or anything someone would love to learn. So whenever you have free time, teach those interested.

Offer Pet Caring Services

The pet industry is growing every year. If you love animals, it makes sense to make money doing something you enjoy. Pet care services you can provide include pet walking, pet sitting, and pet grooming. Actually, there are some people who earn a nice living just playing with pets.

Chapter 6: How to Be Successful at Saving

You will have to make huge investments in life. Apart from that, you may have emergencies to deal with. Without any savings, these situations may force you into borrowing, which can be a lengthy process.

Without question, saving is important. Whether you would like to buy a house, pay for college, or plan for emergencies, savings will be a cushion when the going gets hard.

Many have trouble saving because they believe they don't earn enough. But remember, you can't build a city in a day. The same is true with saving. Make small contributions every month and soon, the money will add up.

Below are some tips you can follow to be successful at saving money:

Make a plan – having a plan helps you know your destination. It also enables you to find the best road to take. So before you begin saving, make a plan. How much will you save every month? Will you use this money for college, retirement, or emergencies? Whatever your goal, ensure it's clear and explicit. That way, you will be able to stick to your plan. And you will increase your chances of success.

Make savings an expense – we have a tendency to fulfill immediate needs first. And we do this while neglecting the future, believing it will sort itself out when the time comes. We believe we will save what will remain when we are done spending. Unfortunately, spending never ends. So saving remains a dream.

If you were to treat saving as an essential expense, however, the story would be different. Whether you like it or not, you will have to allocate some money to your savings account.

The rule is to save 10-15% of your net income. If you can do more, that's even better.

Save automatically – to do this, you will need to contact your bank so it can set up an automatic money transfer. The moment you get money in your account, your bank will automatically transfer an agreed amount to your savings account.

By doing this it will help eliminate the temptation of spending money you should have saved.

Saving isn't just about money – for some people, it's difficult to watch their money sit in the bank. If you are this kind of a person, then you are better off investing your money in something. One such thing is to get a house or some form of a fixed asset. The best part is that you may sell this investment later ideally at a profit.

If you are business minded, you may even invest your savings in a business. However, before you do this, ensure the business is profitable. Without caution, you may end up losing your money.

Watch your money grow – saving money can be difficult when just getting started. Letting your money accumulate from zero is not a joke.

However, something fun happens when you start saving money and see it grow in your account. You get motivated to keep the momentum. And this helps you achieve your goal faster than you thought.

Reward yourself – you wake up daily and go to work because you know you will get something in the end. This is what's called the Expectancy Theory.

And you can use it too to be successful at saving. First, have a clear goal. For example, you may say you will save $250 every month and reward yourself every time you reach $1000. And when you do reach your $1000 goal, give yourself a reward. Make sure the reward is something you care about.

Chapter 7: Dealing with Debts

A debt is like an albatross around your neck. It drags you down, preventing you from enjoying your life. Without care, debts can accumulate. And you may get a headache thinking of how you will repay them. The worst part is that lenders will expect you to pay back regardless of your situation.

Creating a budget is the first step to ensuring that you will successfully get out of debt. A budget gives you an insight on whether you are spending money on things you don't need. And you can easily put an end to this. At the same time, it also helps you know how much of your income you can allocate to paying down your debts.

Here are more tips on dealing with debts:

Pay high-interest loans first – a high interest loan means you will be paying more every month. To avoid this, pay these kinds of loans first. In addition, you may also consider paying more than the minimum to deal with such loans quickly. Repaying the debt faster will save you some money.

Lower your interest rates – you can also call your lender and ask if he can lower your interest rate. This will reduce the amount you have to pay although it may not be much. And don't be afraid to do this. You are a profit center for your lender. Even with a lower interest, your lender will still be making money, which is better than losing you to a competitor with lower interest rates.

Avoid borrowing – for some, borrowing can become an addiction. Even when they do not need to borrow, you will still see them doing it. If you are guilty of this, you need to change your attitude. And a budget can help you do this.

With it, you will see that you are spending money on non-essential things.

Have emergency funds – this is an easy way to keep yourself out of debt. When an emergency hits, you will just use this instead of borrowing. So there is no chance of multiplying your debts.

The rule is to have an emergency fund of at least $1,000.

Get rid of credit cards – these can seem like a convenient way of financing your expenditure when broke. But you know too well they are bait. Without care, they can increase your debt. To eliminate the temptation of ever using them, get rid of them. Your emergency fund should be your new credit card.

Stick to your budget – like I said, budgeting is important if you want to get out of debt. Now that you have it, stick to it. You must do your best to avoid spending more than what your budget allows. That will leave you with money for the settlement of your debts. Also, spending more than you planned means you will have to get more money from elsewhere, which could be another debt.

Cut costs – I gave you some things you can do to cut costs in Chapter 3, so use them. Needless to say, reducing your costs will leave more money in your pocket, which you can use towards paying down your debts.

Make more money – this is another great option for getting out of debt. There is a list of things you can do to increase your income in Chapter 5.

Conclusion

As you saw in this book, making a budget plan is easy. You just need to master how it's done. Once you do that, you'll enjoy all the benefits that come with it.

As a reminder, never get tired of tracking your expenses as well as incomes. This is the key to budgeting. If you get lazy and give up, you will create a budget, but it will have flaws. To make the tracking process easy, have a notebook and a pen ready all the time. If that's too old for you, a note-taking app in your phone is a great alternative.

If you live with others, ensure that they are included in the budgeting process. Their involvement will guarantee commitment to the budget.

In some situations, budgeting may mean changing your lifestyle. This is necessary to make the budget work and ensure that you have enough money for necessities. So if there is a need for change, don't fight it. It will lead to a better life.

When you finally create your first budget, celebrate it. You are now among the 34% who make budget plans.

I wish you financial success!

About the Author

Dr. Usman is an MD, now pursuing his post-graduation degree. As a medical doctor, he has deep insight in all aspects of health, fitness and nutrition.

He is a certified nutritionist and a personal trainer. With these qualifications, he has helped countless people reach their health, fitness and weight loss goals.

Dr. Usman is an avid researcher with 20+ publications in internationally accepted peer reviewed journals.

He is an accomplished writer with more than 5 years of writing experience. In this time, he has produced countless blogs, articles and research work on topics related to health, fitness and nutrition.

He is a published author with more than 100+ books published and several more in the pipe line.

Finally, he runs his own blog and posts health, fitness and nutrition related articles there regularly. You can visit his blog at http://hcures.com/

Check out some of the other JD-Biz Publishing books
Gardening Series on Amazon

Download Free Books!
http://MendonCottageBooks.com

Health Learning Series

Country Life Books

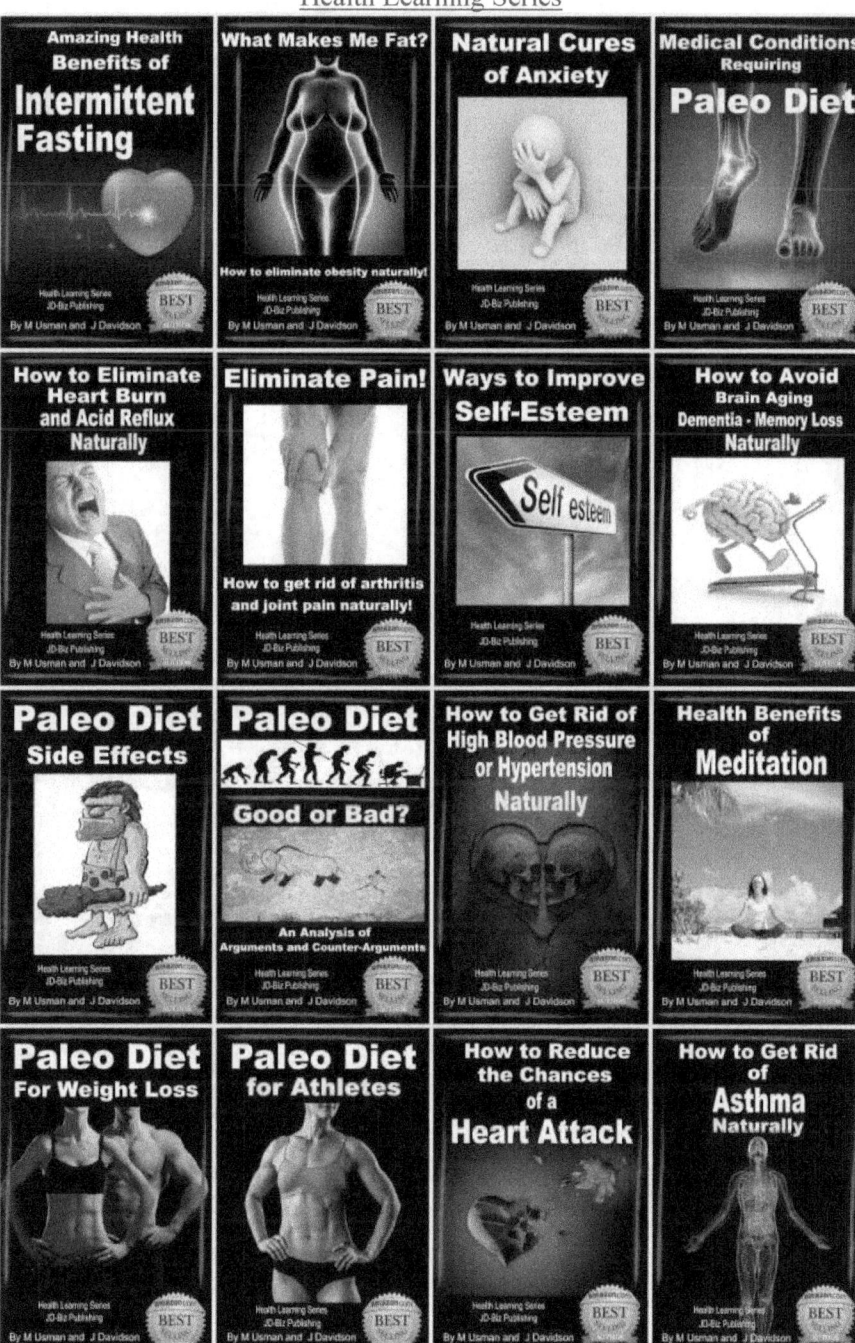

Learn To Draw Series

Entrepreneur Book Series

Our books are available at

1. Amazon.com

2. Barnes and Noble

3. Itunes

4. Kobo

5. Smashwords

6. Google Play Books

Download Free Books!
http://MendonCottageBooks.com

Publisher

JD-Biz Corp

P O Box 374

Mendon, Utah 84325

http://www.jd-biz.com/